# Life Lease

## *A tool for senior housing*

Bryan Law

Fox College of Business

First edition: February 2021

Fox College of Business

# Disclaimer

Fox College of Business and Bryan Law are not engaged in rendering legal, accounting, real estate, or other professional services. This book should not be relied upon as providing such advice. We strongly urge that you seek professional advice prior to acting on the information contained herein.

The information contained herein has been obtained from sources which we believe are reliable, but we cannot guarantee its accuracy or completeness. Fox College of Business, Bryan Law, and every person involved in creating this book disclaim any warranty as to the accuracy, completeness, and currency of the contents of this book. We also disclaim all liability in respect of the results of any action taken or not taken in reliance upon information in this book.

# Preface

Life lease is a relatively new concept in some jurisdictions. Most people, including real estate brokers and lawyers, may not be familiar with the operations of a life lease, and some people have never heard about it. Since it is not common in many areas, there is a lack of legislation to protect consumers.

However, the need for life lease communities has significantly increased due to the baby boomers. This is because most of the baby boomers can afford life-lease style living and would buy them for their retirement life.

There are different life lease sponsors in the market. Although most of them are non-profit organizations, the prices, quality and services vary among them. I hope this book can help consumers select the right life lease community and provide the sponsors with some ideas to improve their business models.

# Bryan Law BSc, LLM, LLD

A well-known author, consultant, and educator in Canada, Bryan has a diversified professional background.

Bryan is a management consultant with more than 20 years of experience. He is also a legal researcher in various areas, including contract law, environmental law, human rights law, labour law, privacy law, and real estate law.

Different education institutions have hired Bryan to provide his expertise in business management, law, and real estate. Bryan has authored over 20 books in various disciplines, including real estate, fiction, mathematics, human rights, creative problem-solving, franchising, employment law, Feng Shui, and more.

Bryan's wide-ranging knowledge and professional experience, coupled with humorous presentation skills, have placed him in demand as a professional speaker as well.

# Table of Contents

# 1: Introduction

The types of real estate ownership and governing laws vary in different countries; they may not be the same among different provinces or states in the same country. In common law countries, the doctrine of tenure and estates describes how a person holds a freehold estate in land as an absolute owner or a right to possess (not own) subject to payment, such as paying a fee after a period of time. In other countries, most of them have property laws to govern the ownership of land.[1]

In Canada and the United States, most of the lands are under fee simple, which is a right to use for an unlimited time and the highest possible form of ownership interest that can be held in real property.[2] In the United Kingdom, many landowners are still holding their land under a 'leasehold' interest, which is an interest for a fixed period of time. A nominal

---

[1] "Land tenure", Wikipedia, last accessed February 21, 2021, https://en.wikipedia.org/wiki/Land_tenure

[2] "Fee simple", Wikipedia, last accessed February 21, 2021, https://en.wikipedia.org/wiki/Fee_simple

fee is usually payable to renew the 'lease' after that period.

In other non-common law countries, there is legislation to govern land ownership to offer protection to land ownership. For example, land in China is basically state-owned or collectively owned, and all mineral resources, waters and sea areas belong to the State. Individual landowners are protected subject only to the government's expropriation.[3]

## Owners and Tenants

Basically, one may hold real property as either the owner or the tenant. Each has its pros and cons. An owner holds the real property for an unlimited time. If the owner is an individual and dies, the ownership will be passed to the estate and inherited by the successors. If the owner is a corporation, its ownership period is endless, as a corporation will never die unless it is dissolved. That

---

[3] "Property Law of the People's Republic of China", last accessed October 21, 2023, http://www.npc.gov.cn/zgrdw/englishnpc/Law/2009-02/20/content_1471118.htm

is why most investment properties are held by corporations, as only a corporation can fully depreciate the property and make the recapture of depreciation insignificant after a long holding period, say 100 years.

An owner has full control of the real property as long as the action is legal. For example, the owner has the right to renovate the property, lease it out to a third party, demolish it, or change its use within the allowed zoning uses. An owner can also enjoy the appreciation in the value of the real property during inflationary periods. There are tax sheltering tools for the owner to enjoy, too. An owner may use the property to apply for a mortgage and assign the leases of the property when it is sold to a third party.

A tenant has a limited term to enjoy a property as stated in the lease, or it is a month-to-month tenancy that a landlord may terminate at any time unless it is protected by law. A tenant may not have the right to sublet the property to a third party unless the landlord must allow it by law and will not have the right to claim the appreciation of the real property. A tenant may also be restricted from modifying or renovating the property without the landlord's consent.

On the other hand, an owner needs to pay a significant amount of initial capital to buy the property and be liable for paying the lender if a mortgage is arranged. An owner will also have to pay realty taxes, fire insurance and maintenance expenses for the property. Although the risk is low, an owner will have to bear the liability of a decrease in property value and a negative rental income cash flow when there is a vacancy.

The initial cost of a tenant is low; usually, it is only a deposit of one month's rent or two. A tenant does not have to maintain the rental property, at least not to administrate the work. A tenant is not liable for any mortgage payments in arrears or negative capital growth of the property value over time. A tenant has the flexibility to move out from the property without incurring a high cost of commission and legal expenses to buy and sell properties.

A life lease is halfway between the ownership and tenancy arrangement, with mixed advantages and disadvantages.

## What is a Life Lease

Life leases apply only to residential properties. A life lease is a form of tenancy arrangement that gives the leaseholder a right to reside in the property for an extended period of time, usually not less than 50 years and commonly for the life lease holders' whole lifetime. Unlike ordinary commercial and residential tenancies, the life lease holders cannot be corporations and can only be individuals.

Although a life lease is a tenancy, its arrangement makes it a special type of tenancy so that the laws govern residential tenancies that may not apply to a life lease. For example, in most jurisdictions, life leases are not regulated by residential tenancy law. The rights, obligations and liabilities between a sponsor and the leaseholders are governed by the life lease they signed. That is, only contract law will apply. Therefore, more and more governments are considering passing legislation to deal with life leases to protect the leaseholders.

A life lease community is usually developed and managed by the same organization. It sells the life lease interests to individuals and stays as the property manager to manage the community.

## Life Lease vs Condominium

A life lease is similar in concept to condominium ownership. A condominium unit owner can reside in the unit unlimitedly but will have to pay the realty taxes, fees for the use of common areas and maintenance. A life lease is the same; the owner of a life lease will have to pay for all those expenses.

Unlike a condominium unit owner, a leaseholder under a life lease does not confer an ownership stake in the property; instead, the leaseholder owns an interest in the property that allows them the right to live in the unit for an agreed period, often longer than their lifetime.

The owners of condominium units can form the board of directors of that condominium complex. The board of directors can make decisions on the rules and regulations of the condominium, how and when the major repairs or maintenance are done, and change the property management company once their contract expires. Life lease holders do not have such rights.

# 2. Senior Housing Choices

Most life leases, if not all, are made for seniors. This is because the style of life leases fits the requirements of senior living. Depending on the seniors' needs and preferences, there are other housing options for seniors to select. They offer different types of features, support or services.

**Independent Living**

Seniors, especially the healthy ones, can opt to stay in their existing homes. It may be a detached house or any freehold property. If needed, they can modify the property to meet ongoing personal requirements (such as wheelchair accessibility issues) and secure appropriate at-home services. They can also move into a condominium unit and avoid many maintenance demands found in freehold properties while enjoying added security, organized social activities and other amenities. However, modifications to the unit to meet personal requirements are restricted by the condominium rules and regulations.

## Co-housing and Co-living

Co-housing involves sharing a home with a friend or family member, and co-living is the concept of sharing a property with some biologically unrelated people or strangers. The settings of the two types are basically the same.

Sharing a home can reduce the individual's living costs, such as property taxes, utilities, insurance and maintenance. If it is a rental property, it can reduce the rental costs. Recently, more and more corporations entered the co-living market by providing quality housing to renters. The target markets are young adults and the working class in metropolitans.

Co-living can also provide additional mutual benefits to the occupants, like companionship, help with daily tasks and extra support in case of an emergency. All of them are important to seniors. It is difficult to say it may be easier to arrange co-housing than co-living or vice versa. It depends on the senior's background – do they have family and friends nearby who are willing to share a home with them?.

This option becomes more popular as it saves living costs by having two or more family generations residing in a single home, especially when the family size is small. Since more and more families have only one child, this option is easier to arrange than before, when most families have two or more children at the time.

**Co-operative Housing (Co-ops)**

There are two types of co-op housing projects. It can either be equity co-operatives, which are with share capital or non-profit co-operatives, which are without share capital. Co-ops are registered corporations that provide housing in return for a share in the maintenance or other tasks. Some co-op housing projects cater specifically to seniors and are seniors-only buildings.

A co-op property is owned by a corporation, and its members have a lease for a specific housing unit and may be permitted to acquire a share in the corporation in the case of an equity co-op. There are co-op housing projects built for students, women and artists. Of course, there are some for seniors.

Co-ops are member-controlled corporations managed by a board of directors consisting of elected persons from the membership. Members pay a monthly housing charge to cover the mortgage, if there is one, and operating costs. Most non-profit co-ops get funding from the government and offer a mix of market-value units and geared-to-income units. For-profit co-ops may distribute any surplus that they generate to their members, but non-profit co-ops cannot.

**Supportive Housing**

Supportive housing refers to residential rental properties with access to services like entertainment, housekeeping, personal support, healthcare, and meals. Most supporting housing operators are non-profit organizations; many of them are religious bodies. There are also for-profit organizations providing supportive housing to seniors who can afford higher living costs.

Residents in supportive housing usually pay market rents and additional fees for the services provided unless it is a subsidizing housing project. Depending on the business model of the operators, the additional fees for the services can be available at market price, reduced costs, or for free. A non-profit organization may also charge fees at market price.

**Retirement Homes and Communities**

Retirement communities can be operated by for-profit and non-profit organizations, too. They offer accommodation and various lifestyle options for active seniors. Retirement communities may consist of retirement homes and other facilities, such as condominium units for sale and commercial space. They typically include tenant and buyer selection restrictions such as age regarding occupancy.

Most retirement homes are rental properties and offer two levels of service: independent living and assisted living. Independent living is like living in a condominium, whereas assisted living is the supportive style mentioned above. Residents of retirement communities will have to enter into a residency agreement setting out specifics of the accommodation and level of services provided. The costs of living vary mainly depending on the facilities and the level of service and support offered.

**Long-term Care**

Long-term care facilities provide accommodation, care, services, meals and programs to seniors who need assistance. In most jurisdictions, they are regulated in accordance with government policies. Admission to a long-term care facility usually has to be authorized by the authority unless it is privately run without government funding.

Most basic services in long-term care facilities are paid for by the government, including accommodation, meals, laundry, furnishings, social and recreational activities, and, most importantly, nursing care. Other services are unfunded services and are payable by the resident. For example, the basic accommodation fee may include a ward but not the additional cost of a private room and cable TV. Furthermore, unfunded services could include medications, dental services, vision care and transportation, depending on individual circumstances. Some retirement communities may also offer long-term care facilities on a private pay basis. However, they may not be the same as long-term care facilities and may limit their care services to assisted living levels.

**Life Leases**

The concept of life leases may be new to some countries, but they have been in existence in North America for several decades. Life lease communities are typically developed by religious, charitable, non-profit or ethnic organizations. Residents pay an upfront fee to buy the right to live in the property for a specific period, usually over 50 years or for life. They will have to pay the monthly payments for the maintenance of the property, too.

# 3. Characteristics of Life Leases

In life-lease housing, the owner of the property is called the sponsor. A sponsor develops the project, sells the occupancy right to the buyers (the leaseholders), and creates a life lease. The buyers of life leases do not own the properties; the sponsors do. The sponsor gives life lease holders an interest in that property only. The life lease interest provides the holder with the right to occupy (live in) a unit rather than own the unit.

## Senior Homes

Life-lease communities target seniors as their occupants. That is because life leases provide extended lease terms for the seniors to live in the property, which are often longer than their lifetime. Therefore, the most significant advantage of a life lease that seniors can get is peace of mind. They can reside on the property as long as they wish.

Like condominium unit owners, the life lease holders pay a lump-sum purchase price to buy the right to own the lease and then continue to pay property taxes and monthly maintenance fees. The prices set for life leases are usually similar to the same-sized condominium units in the neighbourhood.

Since a life lease is not a true type of ownership of real estate, the life lease holder may not be able to sell the interest to a third party unless the new buyer satisfies the eligibility of the life lease community. Depending on the type of life lease ownership, the value of the resale life lease interest may not be the market value; it may be more or less than the market value or even have no value at all. The life lease holder may also have to pay a pre-agreed penalty to the sponsor when they sell their interest.

Unlike real estate ownership, life leases may not be eligible for applying for mortgages. Some governments and financial institutions may have programs to assist seniors in buying life leases. However, the application requirement, process, and amount available to the buyer may not be the same as conventional mortgages.

## Basic Terms and Conditions

The life lease agreement should spell out what kind of maintenance and services are included in the monthly fee and how they are calculated. Besides building maintenance, most sponsors will provide lawn mowing, landscaping, snow, and garbage removal services. Services and maintenance may also include changing furnace filters, fixing electrical wiring or plumbing systems, and security systems such as CCTV monitoring the exterior of the home. Some can provide surveillance inside the homes while life lease holders are away and give their consent in advance.

The sponsors may also provide other services, including housekeeping, laundry, transportation, meals, help with bathing, reminders to take medication and other health or medical supports. Such additional services may be included in the monthly fees or may be offered on an optional basis for an extra cost. All such options and their corresponding fees should be clearly stated in the life lease contract.

Some life lease projects offer a specific religious or cultural environment. Buyers are often attracted by a life lease that provides services in their mother tongue other than English, programs and meals that are specific to a culture, or a particular religious belief and ceremonies. All these services should be stated in the agreement as a condition for buying the life lease, especially for new constructions to be built.

## New Construction

Suppose the life lease community is a new building to be constructed. In that case, the occupants are usually required to pay a deposit to reserve their spots and make further deposits as construction proceeds.

For example, the life lease may be sold for $100,000. Since the property is not constructed yet, the buyers are just required to pay $25,000 (25% of the full price) to secure the spots. They may be required to pay another 25% upon the sponsor obtaining the building permit, 25% upon completion of the foundation and the remaining 25% upon completing the building and getting approval for the occupancy permit.

In some jurisdictions, new homes are covered under a certain type of new home warranty program. However, life leases for new homes may not be eligible for such a new home warranty. Buyers should find it out before committing to buy. If a new home warranty does not apply, buyers should seek some kind of warranty from the sponsor and state it in the life lease agreement. The deposit paid to the sponsor is not protected by insurance in case the sponsor goes bankrupt if the new life lease project is not covered under a new home warranty. Again, professional and legal advice should be sought when dealing with new construction life lease projects.

**Length of the Lease**

Depending on the jurisdiction and common practice, a life lease can be a fixed term or a flexible term. A typically fixed lease term is 50 years. Most life leases do not expire at the end of the term, but they will have to be renewed if the occupant wants to stay beyond the term.

A flexible term lasts until either the end of the leaseholder's lifetime or the leaseholder decides to move out. If a leaseholder who passes away has a spouse, the life lease is usually transferable to the spouse for the term of the life of the spouse. However, the surviving spouse must meet the sponsor's eligibility criteria, such as age requirements. The spouse may also have to pay a transfer fee.

If a leaseholder passes away and has no spouse, the life lease interest will go to the estate or be terminated if there is no heritor. It depends on the governing law, which will be discussed in the section below. A buyer should carefully review the life lease agreement to see how the duration of occupancy is defined for a flexible term and how the renewal process is done for a fixed term.

## Governing Law

Unless there is legislation in your region that governs life leases, all the terms and conditions of a life lease are governed by contract law. That is, all the provisions set out in individual life-lease agreements would apply in the event of a dispute before the courts. Therefore, people should read a life lease agreement closely and seek the advice of qualified professionals, such as accountants and legal counsel, before signing it.

Under contract law, a life lease term can be fixed and terminated upon the death of the leaseholder. That is, the sponsor may get the property back. However, in most life-lease communities, especially those run by non-profit organizations, if a life lease holder passes away, the inheritor usually gets the life lease interest but not the right to occupy the unit. The inheritor can sell the life lease, but they cannot automatically move into the home.

For example, a life lease holder dies at the age of 87, and the inheritor is 59 years old. The life lease community has a rule that only people 60 years old or older may be eligible to live on the property. Still, the inheritor may apply to the life lease sponsor to live in the unit. The life lease sponsor may decide to be flexible and allow the inheritor to continue residing in the property. The inheritor may be required to pay a transfer fee and sign a new life lease agreement with the sponsor.

If the sponsor refuses the application, the inheritor cannot move into the property but can sell it. An administration fee may be charged upon the transfer of interest. Alternatively, the inheritor can wait a year and then apply to move in.

## Benefits of Life Leases

The biggest attraction of life-lease properties is the peace of mind of the seniors. They do not have to move out from the community as long as they can live independently; the life lease community also provides services and features to seniors that are not available in the condominiums.

To summarize, people choose life leases for their housing needs because:

1. Life leases may be more affordable than purchasing the ownership.
2. They may be exempted from certain types of taxes, such as land transfer tax and duties.
3. The residents have fewer home maintenance responsibilities.

4. Most residents would have access to organized social and recreational programs.
5. Many life-lease communities offer care and meal services.
6. Since most life-lease communities are run by religious or cultural groups, and the occupants are mainly seniors, they have a sense of community and belonging.

# 4. Types of Life Leases

It does not matter whether the life lease sponsor is a for-profit corporation or a non-profit organization; their business model decides what type of life lease they will offer. The following are some of the typical life leases available in the markets with no law to govern life leases.

## Zero Balance Life Lease

In a Zero Balance life lease, the amount the leaseholder pays upfront is based on the present value of the whole term of a life lease. That is, the leaseholders prepay the rent for the rest of their expected remaining lifetime. The calculation is done by discounting the values of all projected rents in the future to the present value. The number of months used to calculate future rents is based on the leaseholder's life expectancy. The longer their life expectancy, the higher the amount the leaseholders will have to pay.

That is the least expensive form of life lease housing. However, if the leaseholders pass away, their spouse will not be able to stay on the property unless their surviving spouse is also one of the leaseholders. The holder's estate will not inherit the life lease interest; it will return to the sponsor upon the lease holder's death. The same happens when the leaseholders move out of the property. No residual value will be paid to the holders' estate if the leaseholders pass away or decide to move elsewhere, even if it is due to a health issue that forces the leaseholders to leave the property earlier than expected.

Since the life leases expire upon the lease holders' death, their inheritors do not have the right to stay in the property, transfer or sell the lease. The advantage is that inheritors do not have to worry about selling the life leases and do not have to continue paying the monthly fees.

## Declining Balance Life Lease

In a Declining Balance life lease, the amount the leaseholders pay upfront is based on a mix of the market value of the property and the life expectancy of the buyers. The residual value reduces with the increase of the leaseholder's age. The amount the holders or their inheritors will receive declines by a specific scale each year until it reaches zero.

That is the second least expensive form of life lease housing. The life lease holders' right to occupy the property lasts for their lifetime, even after the residual value has declined to zero. If the leaseholders pass away or move out, their spouse will not be able to stay in the property unless their surviving spouse is also one of the leaseholders.

As with the Zero Balance life lease, this model will not profit when the real estate values go up. The leaseholders will get the declined value pre-calculated in the life lease agreement according to the life expectancy of the leaseholders. The lease holders' inheritor will not get the life lease interest but the residual value of the property.

**Fixed Value Life Lease**

In a Fixed Value life lease, the amount the leaseholders pay upfront is based on the market value of the property and may be subject to a specific discount due to the life lease nature. The value of the life lease is not tied to the age expectancy or length of occupancy of the leaseholders.

This model is also called the "no gain" life lease, as the leaseholders will get back the exact amount they paid for the life lease with no capital gain, even if the real estate market goes up. The sponsor will purchase the life lease back from the leaseholders or their inheritors for the same amount of money that the leaseholders originally paid for the life lease. The sponsors may retain a percentage of the amount as an administrative and refurbishing fee.

The main advantage of this model is that even if real estate values go down, the leaseholders or their inheritors are guaranteed to get their initial payment back. However, if real estate values go up, the leaseholders or their inheritors will not profit.

Although the leaseholders can get the originally paid money back, this kind of life lease cannot enjoy inflationary appreciation. In other words, the money the leaseholders invested loses its value over time. Again, if the leaseholders pass away or move out, their spouse will not be able to stay in the property unless their surviving spouse is also one of the leaseholders.

**Price Index Life Lease**

In a Price Index life lease, the amount the leaseholders pay upfront is based on the market value of the property and may be subject to a specific discount due to the life lease nature. The value of the life lease is not tied to the age expectancy or length of occupancy of the leaseholders.

The sponsor will increase the original amount paid annually by an inflation index factor, usually the Consumer Price Index (CPI), and pay the increased amount to the leaseholders or their heritors when the leaseholders move out or pass away. The sponsors may retain a percentage of the increased amount as an administrative and refurbishing fee when they pay to the leaseholders.

Although there is a guarantee for the gain in real estate value by using an inflation index, the leaseholders or their heritors will not profit if real estate values go up higher than the increased amount calculated by the sponsor. Of course, if real estate values go down, the leaseholder is guaranteed to have the pre-agreed increased amount.

Again, if the leaseholders pass away or move out, their spouse will not be able to stay in the property unless their surviving spouse is also one of the leaseholders.


## Market Value Life Lease

A Market Value life lease is the most popular type among the five different life leases. In a Market Value life lease, the amount the leaseholders pay upfront is based on the market value of the property and may be subject to a specific discount due to the life lease nature. The value of the life lease is not tied to the age expectancy or length of occupancy of the leaseholders.

The leaseholders can sell their life lease interests at any time. If the leaseholders sell their life lease interest for more than they originally paid for it, the leaseholders make a profit. If the leaseholders sell their life lease interest for less, then they incur a loss. The same applies to the lease holders' inheritors.

Almost all Market Value life leases will allow the leaseholder to transfer the life lease interest to their inheritors. That means the life leases last longer than the life of the leaseholders. Although the holder's inheritors may profit from the sale of the life lease, they may not move into the unit without first applying to the sponsor and meeting the sponsor's eligibility criteria, most likely an age restriction.

The leaseholders and their heritors can opt to sell the life leases in the open market. The sponsor may also assist them by assessing unit value, contacting prospective buyers from the waiting list or brokering the sale. Regardless of the procedure, the sponsor may retain a percentage of the sale price as an administrative and refurbishing fee. If the leaseholders retain a real estate agent to assist them, the brokerage fee will be paid by the leaseholders on top of the administrative and refurbishing fees.

Unlike the other four types of life leases, the value of Market Value life leases will vary according to the real estate market. If the real estate market goes down, the leaseholders or their heritors may have a capital loss unless they keep the property without selling it. However, the leaseholders may not be able to sublet the property if they keep it, or the inheritors cannot move into the property. That may cause them the operating costs to keep the property vacant as they will have to pay the monthly fees as long as they keep the property.

## Conclusion

It does not matter whether the sponsor is a for-profit corporation or a non-profit organization; most of them will pick either the Zero Balance model or the Market Value model.

The Zero Balance model provides the lowest cost for the buyers to own a life-lease property. Although the leaseholders may not get any residual value at the end of the lease term, that will only happen when they pass away or move out of the property after their life expectancy. In that case, they have earned extra 'free rental years' as their occupancy period is longer than their life expectancy. For the sponsors, they do not have to refund the full amount of the life lease interest, and the refund amount is usually meagre.

The Market Value model provides the sponsors more cash flow to build a new life lease community, especially when they are not required to buy back from the life leaseholders. The buyers may get the profit of real estate appreciation when they sell the life lease interest.

# 5. Managing Life Leases

The property management company of a life lease project is usually the sponsor itself. Therefore, the first step to ensure a life lease community can be managed well is to have a well-drafted life lease agreement. While a lawyer can assist a sponsor in using proper legal language to ensure the agreement is enforceable, the sponsor should know the life lease project basics.

## Eligibility

First things first, a life lease community must have a clearly defined eligibility if it is not an open community that allows everyone to live in it. The most common restriction on life lease communities is age eligibility. For new construction, should the age be counted on the day of signing the agreement? On the day that the final payment is paid? On the day that occupancy is granted? Do both spouses need to be qualified for the age requirement? Can the buyers buy it first and wait until they are at the required age to move in? The last question may affect how the price of a life-lease property is calculated.

Many life lease sponsors are religious or cultural organizations; they may have specific requirements to determine eligible leaseholders. They may also impose a certain percentage of leaseholders to be a particular ethnic group, religious group, or cultural group. In some rare cases, a luxury life lease community may require the buyers to have adequate savings or income as proof of ability to pay for the monthly fees.

## Price Setting

A sponsor will have to decide the pricing model of a life-lease project before it is built. The initial value of the property will likely be priced according to similar properties in the same real estate market, that is, at market value. Only the Zero Balance model uses the discounted rent to calculate its value; therefore, establishing the market value is crucial for the other four models.

Suppose a new construction life lease project uses a Zero Balance or Declining Balance model to establish values, and the buyers are allowed to buy the properties first and wait until they are at the required age to move in. In that case, the age used for calculating the life expectancy of the buyers may significantly affect the price of the property. The life lease agreement should state which age will be used – the lease holder's age at the buying time, at the occupancy time, or else.

For using the Price Index model, the name of the index and the announcing authority should be named in the agreement. Different authorities may have used different sets of statistical data, hence producing different index numbers. The calculation method should also be stated if the index in a particular year becomes a negative number.

For all models, the sponsors have to clearly explain, with statistics or formulas, how the value of the life lease property is calculated. For Zero Balance, Declining Balance, and Price Index models, examples should be given to illustrate how the values are calculated.

## Reserve Fund

Like condominium corporations need a reserve fund for major repairs and replacement of their common elements, life lease sponsors also need money for that purpose. Therefore, they will also set up a reserve fund and save money for future capital and significant expenditures such as roof repairs, building exterior finishes, window replacement, asphalt paving, recreational facilities, parking lots, and electrical, heating and plumbing systems. Items covered by the reserve fund for each life lease community may vary depending on its features and services provided.

Once a new life lease community is constructed and occupied, the leaseholders will start paying their monthly occupancy fees. Part of the monthly fees will be contributed to the reserve fund for future use. A reserve fund account will be separately set up for such a purpose. All interest and other income from the reserve fund also form part of that fund. The amount contributed to the reserve fund may be adjusted over time, especially when the amount in the account may not be enough for future repairs and maintenance.

Many jurisdictions do not have legislation to require sponsors to conduct regular reserve fund studies. However, a reserve fund study should be done to determine how much money needs to be put aside each year so that the reserve fund would have enough money to repair the equipment and do the scheduled maintenance. Many sponsors would hire professionals to carry out a reserve fund study; some of them have in-house managers to do the study. Reserve fund studies are usually prepared after three to five years of occupancy and then revised every three to five years.

## Living Arrangements

If a life lease community has a restriction on age, a couple will usually be qualified when one of them meets such a requirement. The age of one spouse should not affect the other's ability to buy the life lease as long as both of them will live in the property.

For example, if one of a couple is 56 years old and the spouse is 30. Since the older spouse meets the age restriction of at least 55 years old, the young age of the spouse will not affect their ability to buy the life lease property under both names as long as they live together in the property. However, when the older spouse passes away, the surviving spouse will not be able to stay on the property even though the surviving spouse is also one of the leaseholders.

Most life-lease communities will not permit life the leaseholders to invite their children or grandchildren to live with them, subject to short-term visits approved by the sponsors. However, some of them allow the family members of the leaseholders who are over 18 to move into the property as caregivers. Of course, that also includes professional support workers.

**Fee Increases**

The monthly fees that life leaseholders have to pay may include the service fee, utilities, insurance property taxes, maintenance costs and reserve fund contribution. It is not purely the rent as in other residential tenancies. Therefore, the law may not be able to limit how much a life lease project can increase monthly fees without asking the sponsors to separate them into different categories.

In fact, the Life Leases Act of Manitoba allows a non-profit sponsor to require the leaseholders to pay their share of the shortfall as a rent increase as the leaseholders' share of budgeted operating costs and contributions to reserve funds. That is, there is no control in the 'non-rent' portion of a life lease because the portion includes expenses such as realty taxes, repair and maintenance that are not controllable by the sponsors. For for-profit sponsors, only the rent portion of the monthly fee is under the rent control guideline.

Since most life lease sponsors are non-profit organizations whose goal is to provide affordable housing to seniors, they will maintain stable and healthy operating expenses to avoid raising fees dramatically. That is why the Manitoba Life Leases Act exempts non-profit sponsors from rent control guidelines. However, to keep the monthly fees low, an adequate reserve fund is required to ensure the life lease community has enough money for future repair and maintenance to avoid a sudden increase in monthly fees. A well-conducted reserve fund study can prevent a miscalculation of such required money.

## Subletting

Many sponsors will not allow the leaseholders to sublet their units unless they are required by law to permit subletting. In instances where sponsors do allow the leaseholders to sublet, they usually require the subtenants to satisfy the sponsor's criteria, such as age requirement or religion fit. Moreover, the subtenants must be able to live independently.

A sublet is not an assignment (a sale of the life lease interest); it is not a full transfer of the life lease interest. The original life leaseholders may be able to get the property back from the subtenant and resume their occupancy. As the subtenants will replace the life lease holders to pay the monthly fees, the sponsor may ask the life lease holders and their subtenants to sign a separate agreement to acknowledge and agree to each party's rights and obligations under the subletting. The original leaseholder may be liable if the subtenant fails to pay the monthly fee.

## Common Rules

Managing life-lease communities is like managing condominium complexes; there are rules and regulations for the property managers to govern the residents' behaviour. Although most life lease communities permit residents to keep pets, they often have restrictions on the breeds, sizes and weights. Service animals, which have been trained to perform tasks that assist disabled people, are not classified as pets.

Most life-lease communities do not allow residents to smoke in the common areas of the property, both indoors and outdoors. Suppose the use of marijuana is legal in your jurisdiction. In that case, it should be prohibited both indoors and outdoors, including the lease holder's own unit, unless it is for medical use or the life lease property is a detached structure. That kind of rule is more common in apartment-style buildings than in townhouse-style structures.

The renovation of the life lease holder's unit may also be restricted. The sponsors may want the leaseholders to renovate the property with particular specifications to maintain the building's quality and ensure that the renovation will not cause other residents any inconvenience, especially in apartment-style buildings. For example, the noise and dust produced by the works will affect the neighbours in an apartment building more easily than the other types of structures. Usually, renovation hours are from 11 a.m. to 7 p.m.

## Termination

A life lease may be ended early, before the death of the leaseholders. It may be due to the health issue of the leaseholders so that they cannot live independently without presenting a safety risk to themselves or the neighbours, non-payment of monthly maintenance fees, continued violations of the rules and regulations of the life lease community, or else.

Depending on the scenario, most life lease agreements usually give the sponsor the ability to end the life lease with a one-month notice if the sponsor determines that the resident is no longer able to live independently. The residual value, if any, will be calculated accordingly. If the reason for moving out is not health-related, the notice period may be longer, and the administration fee charged may also be higher.

Early termination of a life lease may cost the leaseholders a significant amount of money when the life lease is a Zero Balance or Declining Balance model. The residual value of the life lease will be zero in the former case and minimal in the latter case. If it is a Market Value model and the real estate market is bad, it will also incur a loss. Therefore, it is crucial to have a detailed clause in the life lease agreement to state the costs and how it is calculated so that the buyers are fully aware of such fees before accepting the life lease agreement.

**Dispute resolution**

In most jurisdictions, the residential tenancy law may not apply to life leases. As a result, there may not be any special tribunal to adjudicate the disputes between the sponsor and the leaseholders; they may have to go to the courts.

Since life leases are private contracts, the lease agreements are the private law for the sponsors and leaseholders to use as references. Unless there is a law to govern life leases, the agreements signed contain all the rights and obligations that both parties have to honour. That is why a life lease agreement must be clearly and detailedly written.

Like the bylaws of condominiums, the provisions in life leases are the framework of the governance of the community, but the rules and regulations affect the residents' daily lives more. Therefore, many disputes between the sponsors and leaseholders are related to the rules, regulations and services.

Sponsors should have a dispute resolution policy in place to make fair and reasonable decisions for the disputes. Some sponsors have a resident's committee, consisting of leaseholder members and sponsor representatives, to deal with the conflicts. If the decision made by the committee is not satisfied by the leaseholders, there may be a system for them to address the issues to the board of directors, and the board's decision is final by the sponsor.

If the leaseholders are still not satisfied with the resolution results or the board's decision, they may seek outside assistance. Depending on the nature of the disputes, the leaseholders may go to a tribunal, such as the Human Rights Tribunal, or the courts for legal proceedings.

# 6. Life Leases Acts

There is currently no legislation in the US and the UK to govern the contents of life leases. However, the governments have regulations to deal with the nature of life leases, such as mandatory registration or a life lease subject to the taxes related to real estate conveyance.

## The Need for Legislation

Manitoba is the only province in Canada that has legislation to govern life leases. Other provinces, such as Saskatchewan, are also considering enacting legislation to regulate certain aspects of life lease housing developments. Ontario also introduced Bill 155 on September 20, 2017, which proposes a new law to regulate life leases. Although Manitoba's Life Leases Act only applies to life leases in Manitoba, we can use it as a reference when one has to consider a life lease as an alternative to the existing housing option.

A law to govern life leases will aim at protecting consumers by setting the minimum standards that life lease sponsors must follow. It may stipulate what kind of information a new life lease project sponsor must deliver to the prospective buyers, prohibit life lease projects on leased lands, restrict the purchase price and other payments, and allow life lease buyers to cancel their agreement under certain conditions.

The law may also set rules for subletting the life leases, dealing with delayed occupancy of new life lease projects, reporting financial information annually, using reserve funds, refunding procedures, setting up a resolution committee, regulating the mortgage, and setting up a board of directors to include the leaseholders.

## A Glance of Manitoba Life Leases Act[4]

As of February 2021, Manitoba is still the only province in Canada with legislation to govern

---

[4] "The Life Leases Act", Government of Manitoba, last accessed October 21, 2023, https://web2.gov.mb.ca/laws/statutes/ccsm/l130e.php

life leases. It may also be the only jurisdiction in the world to have a law to deal with life leases. Therefore, it is worth knowing their law and using it as a reference when we have to deal with life leases on our own. Both sponsors and leaseholders may insert some clauses in the life lease agreement to establish the right or obligation that the Manitobans have under their law.

## Cooling-off Period

In Manitoba, all sponsors of new life lease projects must insert a prescribed statement in their agreements to allow the buyers to cancel the agreement within seven days after the day on which the life lease or offer to lease signed by the buyer is given to the sponsor. The buyer does not have to provide any reason to cancel the agreement, and this is called the "cooling-off" period.

Suppose a sponsor fails to include such a statement of cancellation rights in the life lease or is not in the prescribed form.[5] In that case, the seven-day period does not begin until the sponsor gives the

---

[5] "User's Guide To Life Lease Forms", Government of Manitoba, last accessed October 21, 2023, https://www.gov.mb.ca/cca/rtb/ot/lifelease/usersguide.html

leaseholder the prescribed statement of cancellation rights.

For an existing life lease project and the buyer is an assignee, the seven-day period does not begin until all the following happen: (i) the assignor signs the assignment, (ii) the assignee signs the assignment, (iii) the sponsor gives the written consent to the assignment, and (iv) the sponsor provides the assignee with the prescribed statement of cancellation rights.

## Refund Fund

At least 95% of the purchase price (called the entrance fee in Manitoba) has to be refundable if the sponsor is not a non-profit organization or the term of the lease is for the leaseholder's life. If an entrance fee is refundable, the sponsor must establish a fund to secure the sponsor's obligations to refund entrance fees and shall appoint a trustee to administer the account.

If the entrance fee is refundable, the sponsor must disclose to the prospective buyer the minimum amount that will be contributed to the refund fund by the sponsor. The sponsor is then required to contribute to the refund fund an amount not less than the minimum amount stipulated in the sponsor's disclosure to the leaseholders before the occupancy date of the life lease complex.

## Failure to Give Possession

For new life lease projects, delayed closing is only allowed for a period of 30 days. Suppose a sponsor fails to give vacant possession of the life lease property 30 days after the projected completion date stated in the agreement. In that case, the buyer can cancel the agreement by written notice to the sponsor before the sponsor gives vacant possession of the unit.

Once vacant possession cannot be given to a leaseholder on the scheduled closing date, the leaseholder may give the sponsor early notice of cancellation during the 30-day period after the projected completion date. However, the cancellation is effective only at the end of the 30-day period and only if, by that time, the sponsor has not offered the leaseholder immediate and vacant possession of the rental unit. A leaseholder who cancels a life lease under this scenario is entitled to a full refund of the entrance fee.

## Annual Meeting

The sponsor of a new life lease project must call a meeting of the leaseholders within 16 months after the occupancy date of the complex. For existing life lease projects, the meeting must be held no later than six months after the end of each fiscal year of the sponsor.

The purpose of the meeting is to present the financial statements and hear any representations by leaseholders respecting the financial statements or the operation of the life lease community. The sponsor must give each life leaseholder a written notice of the time and place of the meeting at least 30 days and not more than 50 days before the meeting.

## Limitation

The Act disallows a non-profit organization to own more than one life lease project, except acting as the role of a property manager.

When a life lease project is based on a condominium complex, the sponsor cannot sell a life lease condominium unit without giving the leaseholder of that unit a Right of First Refusal. Such a Right of First Refusal shall be exercisable before the unit is offered for sale to a third party. The leaseholder shall have the right to purchase the life lease unit at a price not exceeding the price agreed with the third party and on terms that are not less favourable than the third party's.

## Rent Increase

Both for-profit and non-profit sponsors must give a three-month written notice to the leaseholders to increase the rent. The notice must tell the leaseholders how the present monthly rent is separated into different categories and how the new rent is spread over those categories.

The annual rent increase guideline of the Manitoba Residential Tenancies Act does not apply to non-profit life lease projects. Although non-profit sponsors have no motivation to raise rents for profit, the occupancy costs may increase every year, especially when the repair and maintenance costs increase significantly. Therefore, the leaseholders may still ask the Residential Tenancies Branch to review the monthly fee increase.

For-profit life lease projects are subject to the annual rent increase guideline. Therefore, the notice for rent increase must also fulfill the annual rent increase guideline requirements, including the amount of the guideline and a statement that the leaseholder has the right to object to the rent increase. If the sponsor wants a higher increase, they must apply to the Residential Tenancies Branch for approval.

However, the annual rent increase guideline does not apply to for-profit life lease projects built and occupied after April 9, 2001; those units are exempt for 15 years. If the life lease project was built and occupied after March 7, 2005, the units are exempt from the guideline for 20 years. Moreover, the guideline also does not apply to life-lease units renting for more than a certain amount. The amount may change every year.

Assignment

Under the Act, a leaseholder may assign a life lease unless the lease provides that at least 95% of the entrance fee paid in respect of the lease is refundable and there is a provision in the lease that prohibits assignment.

In other words, if there is no refundable entrance fee or there is no provision in the life lease to disallow assignment, then the leaseholders shall have the right to assign.

Conflict with Other Acts

It is worth noting that, like the residential tenancies law in many jurisdictions, the Manitoba Life Leases Act states that if there is a conflict between the Life Leases Act and any other law, the Life Leases Act prevails.

That will have to be amended sooner or later, as it may create problems. For example, the Manitoba Human Rights Code also states that,

> *Unless expressly provided otherwise herein or in another Act of the Legislature, the substantive rights and obligations in this Code are paramount over the substantive rights and obligations in every other Act of the Legislature, whether enacted before or after this Code.*[6]

---

[6] "The Human Rights Code", Government of Manitoba, last accessed October 21, 2023, https://web2.gov.mb.ca/laws/statutes/ccsm/h175e.php

What if an issue involves both the Life Leases Act and the Human Rights Code, but their stipulations contradict each other. Which one will supersede the other one? Similar conflicts may also apply to life lease projects based on condominiums. Should the condominium rules and regulations, which are supported by the Condominium Act, prevail over the Life Leases Act?

**A Fair Framework**

Although the Manitoba Life Leases Act only applies to life lease projects in Manitoba, it is a useful reference for the sponsors to set up their business model. It is also a good reference for the buyers to understand their rights and seek appropriate protections in the life lease agreement when there is no law to govern life leases in their areas. It is a tool for non-profit organizations outside Manitoba to set up a fair and reasonable life lease community.

By referencing the Manitoba Life Leases Act as the strictest control on life lease projects, we can still develop some business models that are win-win for both the sponsors, either for-profit or non-profit organizations, and leaseholders. On the other hand, if the business models can work in Manitoba and comply with its Life Leases Act, those models can also be carried out in other jurisdictions, especially those without any law to govern life leases.

# 7. Business Models

Thanks to the baby boomers, senior housing has been in great demand in recent years. Different senior housing options have been discussed in Chapter 2. If the seniors can live independently, they are not qualified for a long-term care home. If they want services such as meals and health care, independent living is not the choice. A life-lease property can give them more privacy than co-housing does.

Compared with co-operative housing, life-lease housing does not have low-income requirements, and the features are usually better than co-operative housing. Life-lease housing also provides peace of mind to the leaseholders to live in the property for life. On the other hand, the leaseholders may also profit from the real estate appreciation, which is not available in supportive housing and retirement homes. That is why life lease projects are more and more popular in many areas, and it may take more than a year to wait for a vacant unit to be available.

The sponsor of a life lease project may be a for-profit or non-profit organization. Regardless, the two different types of organizations have a common goal – to grow their organization over time. In order to do so, they have to have enough working capital.

Non-profit Business Model

Since the Manitoba Life Leases Act disallows any non-profit organization to own more than one life lease project, except acting in the role of a property manager, operating a property management company is a good source of income for non-profit life lease sponsors. Because of the non-profit nature and image, the property management company run by a non-profit organization may get contracts from other rental property owners more easily than the for-profit ones. Moreover, since life lease communities are usually for seniors, the property management business can also specialize in managing senior homes and retirement communities, which also gives the company a selling edge.

In Manitoba, at least 95% of the purchase price of a life lease property has to be refundable if the sponsor is not a non-profit organization or the term of the lease is for the leaseholder's life. In other words, a non-profit sponsor can sell life leases for a fixed term, say 50 years, and offer no refundable entrance fee.

That can bring more capital, especially cash flow, to a non-profit life lease sponsor by selling the interests without refunds. A lease term of 50 years can give peace of mind to the seniors as 50 years shall be long enough for them to live in the property for life if the age eligibility is set at 60 and even at 55. If the leaseholders still live in the property after 50 years, the life lease can be set to become a month-to-month tenancy, and the leaseholders pay only a nominal rent of $1 per month on top of the monthly operating costs.

The non-refundable entrance fees will give the non-profit sponsors more capital to grow their organization, including expanding their property management business.

## For-profit Business Model

By the same provision of the Life Leases Act mentioned above, for-profit life lease sponsors must refund at least 95% of the purchase price to the leaseholders regardless of the length of the lease term. However, it still provides a good source of capital to the sponsors because it is the sponsor who decides how much money will be kept in the refund fund. The Life Leases Act does not set a minimum amount for a refund fund.

Suppose the life lease community is in a sought-after neighbourhood, and the property is well-maintained. In that case, when the life leaseholders want to sell their interest, they may sell it to a third party at market price (if it is a Market Value model). Alternatively, the sponsor can refund the leaseholders the money at the pre-fixed value and sell it at market price, which is usually higher than the pre-fixed value.

As a result, the money to be placed in the refund fund may be minimal, say, just the value of one unit. It is like one hundred people deposit $100,000 into a bank, but each of them will only get 95% of the money back. The bank gets $10 million in total but will have to keep only $95,000 cash for their customers to withdraw. It will be the most fantastic business for a bank.

Since a for-profit corporation can own more than one life lease project, the sponsor can use that money raised by the sales of the life leases, less the money contributed to the refund fund, to start another life lease project. The snowball will roll bigger and bigger.

On the other hand, since the rent increase guideline does not apply to units renting for more than a certain amount, for-profit sponsors can aim at providing luxury life lease properties to seniors, and the rent can catch up with the market rent without capping by the guideline.

Mixed Business Model

A mixed business model for non-profit sponsors can be based on the business models of non-profit and for-profit sponsors discussed above. First of all, a non-profit sponsor develops a life lease project and builds up a property management company to run the life lease community and manage buildings for other landlords.

The non-profit sponsor can set up a for-profit subsidiary or a sister company, depending on the tax rule and governing law. The profit made by this subsidiary, or the sister company, can be used to develop more than one life lease community and luxury life lease communities or fund the non-profit sponsor in other areas.

Since the for-profit extended arm can own many life-lease communities, it will provide enough properties for the non-profit property management company to manage and grow. Together, both organizations will become bigger and bigger.

~ The End ~